# ABC's of Success

## Timeless Truths

## for

## All Ages

Sissy Scroggins

© 2019
Publisher: **yOur Backyard**
shELAH
Centerville, TN 37033
USA

| | |
|---|---|
| Publications Coordinator: | Lahcen Belkimite |
| Cover Design: | Randall Sandefur |
| Editors: | Erin Murphy Anderson |
| | BJ aka Scanner Eyes |

To Zachary,

    I wrote this book for you before you were born, while you were still in my belly....

                      ~ Love, Mom

This Book of the Law*
shall not depart from your mouth,
but you shall meditate in it
day and night,
that you may observe to do according
to all that is written in it.
For then
you will make your way prosperous,
and then
you will have good success.

~ Joshua 1:8

* Torah—Mosaic Law—Divine Direction

## A big "thank you" to:

**shELAH**, yOur Backyard Publishing, for investing your dedication, professionalism and for continuing to inspire my creativity... for pushing me forward in my writing career.

**Lahcen Belklimite**, Publications Coordinator, for dedicating your brilliance in creative art design and page layout.

**Randall Sandefur**, Creative Designer, for contributing your extraordinary talents to transform my book cover into a masterpiece.

**Erin Murphy Anderson**, Editor & Marketing Specialist, for readily reviewing revisions with your sharp editorial eye.

**BJ** for opening your eyes and heart to scan *ABC's of Success*....

Without you all sharing your wonderful gifts, *ABC's of Success*... would never have reached its maximum potential.

I pray that God richly blesses each one of you.

~ With much love,

**Sissy**

There are no secrets to success.
It is the result of preparation,
hard work, and
learning from failure.

~ Colin Powell

Give up...

At times, prior to Wednesday, October 30, 1996, I had felt like giving up on my dream to become a published author. That crisp fall day years ago, at the Grand Ole Opry in Nashville, Tennessee, however, God used Tony Robbins, a motivational speaker and author, to strengthen my faltering resolve.

Tony's encouraging attitude and words throughout my day working as his personal assistant inspired me to continue with my writing career. I pray that *ABC's of Success...* will likewise encourage the reader to—never give up on his/her dreams and only give in to:

**S**eeing

**U**

**C**ultivating

**C**haracter;

**E**ncouraging

**S**trong

**S**trategies...

to seek and find
God's perfect will
and plan for life.

People rarely succeed
unless
they have fun
in what they are doing.

~ Dale Carnegie

"Read it..."

I smiled as Zachary, my son, three-years-old at the time, shoved the book, *ABC's of Success...*, into my lap and said, "Read it." Zachary had just found the book I had written for him to read when he became a teenager.

"I wrote this book for you before you were born, Zachary, while you were still in my belly...," I explained. "I will read it to you, but you might not understand some of the big words yet."

At first, I felt excited to read his book to him for the first time. But then I thought, *Zachary you're going to run off and play with your fire truck after the first sentence.*

Contrary to my belief, he didn't. Zachary sat with his big, blue eyes wide open, staring up at me until I finished reading every word.

As Zachary grew up, because I wanted him to love to read, I read to him regularly. I knew he could learn how to do just about anything from reading; that it could help him fulfill his dreams. I knew if Zachary loved to read, his opportunities would be unlimited.

Today, I encourage people of all ages to, "Read it..."—and never, ever never give up on your dreams. Success comes as you:

> Never give in,
> never, never, never, never –
> in nothing, great or small,
> large or petty — never give in
> except to convictions of honour and good sense!
>
> ~ Winston Churchill

## Attitude

Your attitude reflects you...
who you are.
Keep a positive attitude
throughout your lifetime.
Sometimes, you will feel down,
but I promise...
if you focus on all the things
you have to be grateful for,
you and others in your life
will be much happier.
As you influence people
you come in contact with,
decide today that
you are going to be
a positive influence
for family, friends, and strangers.
Encourage and lift others up
with your best attitude;
reflecting love.

# B

## Brag

Success does not come by bragging,
but by dedication,
leadership,
and hard work.
Most people do not want to hear
how great you think you are.
Simply be the best you can be,
and give
your most excellent efforts
to whatever you find to do.
Then, when you succeed,
you won't have to brag on yourself.
Others will brag for you.

# C

## Care

Show others that you care.
A small act of kindness, like medicine,
strengthens a faltering heart.
Don't be selfish;
seeking only your own ambitions.
Take time to care for others.
Listen to their hopes and dreams,
and celebrate their accomplishments.
Help others
fulfill their purposes in life....
Lend a helping hand when needed,
and sometimes,
even when someone may not
realize they need help.
This will not only
encourage others,
it will enliven and invigorate you.
Dare to show you care.

# D

## Dream

Just like a flower needs water,
you need a dream.
Give yourself something
to wake up excited about each morning.
Follow your dream.
If you don't have a dream,
don't blame others.
Look in and outside yourself.
Your dream may be small or great.
I believe in dreaming big.
With God,
nothing shall be impossible.
Remember the Bible says—
with faith,
even as small as a mustard seed,
we can say, "Move mountain,"
and that mountain
shall be moved.
With faith,
especially with a lot,
imagine what we might do;
how we could bloom.

## Exercise

Allow time to exercise.
If you don't want to allot
a certain amount of time
each day for exercise,
find creative little ways to move.
Instead of the elevator,
take the stairs.
Pick the parking spot
farthest away from
the building you will enter.
Stretch several times during the day.
Most of all,
for five minutes in the morning
and five minutes in the afternoon,
make a point to breathe in deeply
and let your breaths out slowly.
This will strengthen your lungs and heart,
and lower your stress level.
You'll soon see signs
of healthy progress,
when you make it a priority
to exercise.

## Friend

Treat others the way you want to be treated,
and you'll have no shortage of friends.
Look people in the eye when you talk to them,
and really listen to what they have to say.
Just about everyone loves
someone who listens to them.
Sometimes, just by listening,
you help someone solve their own problem.
Friends come in all shapes, sizes and colors.
They come from different countries,
cultures, backgrounds and educations.
Because it takes
being a friend to have friends,
nurture your friendships
during good times and through the bad.
Being rich or poor does not matter.
A friend loves at all times.

# G

## God

Some might not,
but I believe in God, an infinite Creator,
One above all, Who knows all.
Study the imprints in your palms.
They didn't happen by accident.
God made them that way.
When we seek Him with our hearts,
we see God in things visible
as well as in things that are not.
By putting your trust in God;
in Jesus... you see
that everything happens for a reason.
Remember,
God sees the greater picture.
Only He knows what works best.
He answers our prayers.
Sometimes, His answer may not be
what we wanted, or in the way or time
we expected Him to answer.
But, we can rest assured,
God loves us unconditionally.
As His mysterious ways supersede ours....
He works for our good.

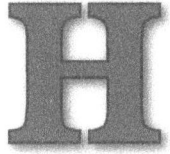

## Happiness

Happiness does not
automatically happen.
Like a work of human art,
being happy takes skill,
determination and practice.
Hundreds of ideas flow
through your mind each day.
Thoughts you decide to focus upon
can make you happy or sad.
Remember, as you think,
you shall be.
Think about good things.
Choose happiness.

# I

## Individual

God made you a unique individual.
He created and empowers you
so that you can
do more than you realize.
Success brings confidence
and feelings of accomplishment.
When other people cannot or fail to help,
never be afraid to go it alone.
If you wait around for someone else,
you may never get anything done.
What's important to you
may not be important to them.
Don't wait.
Start on your project today
and watch what great things
you, an authentic individual,
with God's help,
can make happen.

# J

## Jealousy

Jealousy can mentally drain you
and arouse ugly feelings.
Don't gossip
or let jealousy stand in the way
of your relationships or success.
Be confident and content
within yourself,
then, you won't have to worry
about being anyone else
or wanting their "stuff."
Be thankful
and you won't have room
in your heart for jealousy.
God gives each of us
1440 minutes each day.
Don't waste your valuable moments
feeding the "green-eyed monster."
Instead of jealousy,
choose to be grateful.

# Kindness

Be kind to others.
Don't treat any one person
better than another.
Every opportunity
you can make or take,
show a little kindness.
You'll be amazed
at how awesome you'll feel.
Open virtual and real-life doors
for someone today
and enjoy the bounty of benefits
that come your way.
You may never know how much
you may impact someone
with your
deliberate acts of kindness.
You just might change their day
or entire life for that matter.
When you practice kindness,
you encourage others
to do the same;
to be better.

# L

## Library

Start building your lifelong library today.
Fill it with the Bible
and other books that interest you.
Don't just read your favorite books once.
Read them over and over and over.
Each time,
you'll find something you missed.
If you only learn one thing
from a book, CD, or MP3,
that knowledge has value.
What you read and hear
becomes a part of you.
Even though you might not remember
which book you read something in,
or exactly where
you heard or saw something,
when you need that knowledge,
it will be there for you,
stocked and ready to retrieve
in the library of your mind.

# M

## Money

Don't allow money to control you.
You were born in a land
with great financial opportunities.
Make sure that by the time
you earn your own money,
you're smart enough
to know how to use it.
Don't squander your money thoughtlessly
or spend it foolishly.
Remember to save and invest.
Live within your means.
Use your money wisely
to not only pay your bills
and enhance your life,
but to also help others.
Give when you know
the time to be right.
God loves a cheerful giver.
Remember to do like the Bible says,
provide for your own household.
Honor God first and
let Him lead and control you.
You'll see Him work
things together for your good.

# N

## No

Learn to say "No…."
At times, you need to say, "Yes,"
nevertheless,
you can't say "Yes"
to everything and everyone.
Take time to do
things you need to do.
If you don't, you may become
too tired and worn out
for your own good.
Plain and simple—no means no.
You don't have to give a reason,
especially when
your gut tells you so.
Never ever be afraid to say no.

# O

## Openness

Be open to your loved ones.
Don't hold everything in.
If you keep
Every little thing inside you,
you may become miserable,
and that misery
could take a heavy toll
on you and things you do.
Open yourself up.
Let your friends and family
see, hear and love
the real you.
Be yourself...
I promise that
with openness
in your life,
you will be
so much happier.

# P

## Purpose

Find your purpose in life.
At times,
some people and,
perhaps even you,
may take a little longer
to discover
their God-given purpose.
If you have trouble
realizing or finding yours,
ask yourself:
What am I impassioned about?
What would I love to do?
What could I best invest
my talents into?
As you figure out your niche,
don't fret.
Enjoy the process.
Even before you were born,
God designed for you, in time,
to find and fulfill
His loving will and purpose.

## Question

Never be afraid to ask a question.
That's one of the best ways to learn.
Be direct and specific with what you ask,
and you'll get the best answer.
Throughout history,
many great inventions
began with a question.
"What can I do to
help fix this problem?"
"How can I build that?"
"How can I make something work?"
What have you been wanting to ask?
There's an answer for every question.
You just have to find it.
Be brave....
Ask questions.

## Rest

Make sure you get enough rest.
Research suggests that
most people need seven to eight hours
of sleep each night.
Learn to listen to your body.
If you're feeling too tired during the day,
you may need to increase the time you rest.
Take time to relax when you can.
Get a massage….
Meditate on God's Word.
Too much work or rest, however,
could throw your life off balance.
When you balance work and rest,
your mind, body and health benefit.
You function at your best.

# S

## Smile

Sometimes, even when
you may not feel like smiling...
smile.
Even when you may not feel well
and it may take
a little more effort,
you can do it.
When you smile,
you'll be more approachable
and most of the time,
someone will return the favor.
Why not see
how many smiles
you can give away today?
Then count how many
you receive in return.

## Tomorrow

There are
no guarantees of tomorrow.
Be content in the moment and
happy with what you have today.
Instead of
worrying about tomorrow,
live each moment
with breaths of life,
love and laughter.
If other people choose
to be miserable or grouchy,
don't let their misery
overpower your mood.
Don't wait until tomorrow
to enjoy life.
Live today.

# U

## Universe

God created our universe
with His infinite wisdom.
Remember He spoke,
and with His Word,
light overpowered darkness.
You're a precious part
of His magnificent design.
Your God-given light
shines into the world
and influences others.
Don't let negative energy
flood your part of the universe.
Instead of being dark like the night,
be cheerful
and a blessing to be around.
Spread peace and hope.
Let your words and life
reflect God's universal light.

# V

## Verse

Read Bible verses every day.
Study and plant them
in your heart and brain.
God speaks to us
through His Word.
He longs for us to listen.
When we do, I promise you
that in times of need,
what He says will be there
to help you,
your family, friends and strangers.
In God's perfect time,
verses He brings to mind
will comfort, guide, and protect
not only you,
but also those who
seek Him and heed His Word.

# Work

Always do your part in Church,
in your family,
in your work
and in your community.
A proverb insists,
"Work never hurt anyone."
Don't procrastinate doing any job.
Take that first step of action,
and the other steps will follow.
You will soon mark one job off your list,
and go on to complete the next.
Do the work.
Get busy today.
Do that job you've been putting off.

## X-ray

Learn to have X-ray eyes.
Be on the alert.
Say no to
"get rich quick schemes."
So many scammers in the world
would love to steal your identity
and hard-earned money.
Don't fall prey to predators.
Use your X-ray eyes
and see through
any deal
that looks, feels,
or sounds too
good to be true.

## You

Love yourself.
Don't put yourself down
in front of others.
This could
make them uncomfortable
and they may
shy away from you.
When possible,
try to
look and dress your best
so that you
won't hesitate
when friends or opportunities
come your way.
Take pride in who
God created you
to be…
one of His own.

# Z

## Zone

Zone into
the *ABC's of Success*....
Jump out of your comfort zone.
Don't be afraid to
try something new.
Never stop reading.
Never stop learning
and growing.
Never stop loving others.
In good times
as well as in bad,
even if you
may sometimes want to...,
don't quit.
Give life your best
with everything you've got.

## Recommendations for Your Life-Long Library

* **The Holy Bible**
* **Awaken the Giant Within** by Tony Robbins
* **The Power of Positive Thinking** by Norman Vincent Peale
* **Financial Peace** by Dave Ramsey
* **Crash! Living through the Wreckage** by Carla Moore
* **How to Win Friends and Influence People** by Dale Carnegie

# Final Note to Readers
## from
## shELAH, Publisher

Be brave...
Don't be afraid...
Trust God...

In *ABC's Of Success...*, wise, witty, whimsical characters transport readers through an entertaining educational journey, highlighting every letter of the alphabet. Sissy adapts illuminating illustrations to not only relate timeless, heart-felt, encouraging truths, but to reflect positive practices that help readers pursue "good success" in life. Accented with poignant poetic phrases, she stresses:

* Brag about others; don't focus only on yourself.
* Happiness doesn't just automatically happen.
* Never be afraid to go it alone [because we never are...].
* Jealousy and gossip can mentally drain you and arouse ugly feelings.
* Exercise to help lower stress levels and improve health.
* To have friends, be a friend.
* Remember... you are a part of God's magnificent universe.
* Being negative or positive affects you, as well as those around you. Choose to be positive.
* Do your part in Church, family and community.
* Use X-ray eyes to examine any deal that looks or sounds too good to be true.
* When possible, try to look and dress your best.
* Develop an attitude of gratitude.
* Discover and pursue your God-given purpose for life.
* Never stop learning, growing and loving others.

*ABC's of Success...* encourages readers of all ages that it's never too late to be brave, to face their fears, to trust God and to seek and find His perfect will and plan for life.

Thank you, Sissy.

Sissy embodies the practical, positive principles she lists in *ABC's of Success...* Even though she wrote this timeless, thoughtful book for Zack, her son, it speaks to children, teens and adults of all ages. I as well as others would benefit from practicing them.

~ Cindi Wolk, M.A.
Adjunct in Psychology Department
Tennessee State University (USA)

✳✳✳

Sissy's simple yet encouraging truths in *ABC's of Success...* not only apply to both young and old, they remind us to be and do our best in life. As her book fosters the love and value of reading as an avenue to success, it will prove to be an asset to any family's home library.

~ Ridonna Goodpasture
Office of Special Programs
Classroom/Reading Teacher (TN-USA)

✳✳✳

Written in a simple, yet effective voice, Sissy's book encourages readers to implement genuine, practices in their lives each day. This easy to understand book for all ages offers creative tools to help readers change their lives for the better.

~ Shine King
Dr. Bhimrao Ambedkar University
India

✳✳✳

Thank you, Mom, for encouraging me with *ABC's of Success....* I plan to use the timeless truths, values and morals you have shared with me throughout my lifetime.

~ Love, Zack

www.ingramcontent.com/pod-product-compliance
Lightning Source LLC
Chambersburg PA
CBHW041219240426
43661CB00012B/1087